ISBN 978-0-484-28842-2
PIBN 10244265

This book is a reproduction of an important historical work. Forgotten Books uses
state-of-the-art technology to digitally reconstruct the work, preserving the original format
whilst repairing imperfections present in the aged copy. In rare cases, an imperfection in
the original, such as a blemish or missing page, may be replicated in our edition. We do,
however, repair the vast majority of imperfections successfully; any imperfections that
remain are intentionally left to preserve the state of such historical works.

Progressive Tracts.

No. 4.

APPETITES AND PASSIONS:

Their Origin, and How to Cast Them Out.

A LECTURE,

BY

ANDREW JACKSON DAVIS,

At Dodworth's Hall, N. Y., Sunday Morning, Jan. 25, 1863.

PHONOGRAPHICALLY REPORTED BY ROBERT S. MOORE.

"Fetter strong madness with a silken thread,
Cure ache with air, and agony with words."

A. J. DAVIS & CO.,

OFFICE OF THE HERALD OF PROGRESS,

274 Canal Street, New York.

APPETITES AND PASSIONS:

THEIR ORIGIN, AND HOW TO CAST THEM OUT.

"Fetter strong madness with a silken thread.
Cure ache with air, and agony with words"

It is customary to use old words to put new truths into, though in doing so I think we have failed somewhat. Old bottles impart an old flavor to new wine. Therefore I prefer new words for new thoughts. Ancient peoples used the terms "Devil," "Demon," and "Hell," to express (in as strong language as possible,) the play and seat of the appetites and passions. Those who heard these words frequently failed to understand and comprehend their interior import. The Jews adopted these words, Christians thought a personal Devil was meant, and soon believed in a *place* where countless demons dwell. Modern Christians flounder on the same shoals on account of a misapprehension of terms. It is my present purpose to give you a plan by which you may cast out these educational devils which exist in and haunt the mind through association.

Unitarian and Universalist criticisms prove that orthodoxy is the same as was the mythology of the ancients. The terms "Demons" and "Devils" do not sustain the interpretation which popular orthodoxy gives them. The creed-world goes on its way, not rejoicing, but sadly—believing in the literal interpretation of ancient words. They have not heard the harmonious songs of the universe, nor the "tidings of great joy that shall be unto all people," or they would ascend the mountain summits and gladly contemplate the perpetual beams of divine love and wisdom crowning the surrounding scenery through all the eternity to come. Not having heard these songs nor received these "glad tidings," orthodox Christians have made the journey all the way from Calvary to America a.dark and dismal procession. Many of them require ambulances; for they are patients who have in their minds the sickly dregs of mythology. These creed-riden patients cannot walk; they are rich, and must be taken to church in carriages. On the outside of these fashionable ambulances sit drivers who are beautifully clothed, and who wait until the divinity doctor inside the orthodox hospital gives the final dose of texts with his sugar-coated benediction.

Those who have not joined this melancholy orthodox procession, are born into the present. They partake of the fruits of the trees that grow and flourish to-day. Bitterness to some, but joy and peace to most. Religion misapplied and not digested, or taken in parts and without conglomeration, persecutes its receivers. Great truths dawn gradually. Most minds need sunlight tempered to their short-sighted spiritual eyes.

In the Bible we read of *Sheol*. (I am now biblical.) "Sheol" typifies the human brain. All human minds live in Sheol. All are bilious, and each descends into

Hades—the Liver. A human being, when bilious, dies more than once. The liver is the prepared hell for such. Others go down into *Gehenna*—the Bowels; others to *Tartarus*—the Stomach. Gehenna is the lowest valley—a place for the deposition of that which is gross and corrupt. Evils live in all these "hells" in the human body. Unhappy persons know that there are "unclean spirits" in all these corporeal hells.

Swedenborg, for the most part, wrote philosophically before he became a Spiritualist. He claims to have received an interior notification from the Lord that he was "over-eating" The notice was served upon him just as he was entering upon his spiritual development. He states that the Lord said unto him: "Eat not so much." Is it not astonishing that a philosopher—a man who had written the "Economy of the Animal Kingdom"—should have furnished the necessity of receiving such a notice!

The Bible speaks of "unclean spirits." Jesus cast them out. So, also, did George Combe. Emerson, Parker, and others, cast out devils. Dr. Trall, of this city, also does something in the line of exorcism. So do all reformers in diet and drink. Few men possess the true amulet—the will-power of the immortal spirit—by which personal evils are over-mastered and exorcised. If you do not carefully control your appetites you will surely live in some one or more of these bodily hells—with the fearful privilege or with the necessity of making frequent visits to the others!

There is a lesson in a child's imaginative description of a Satan. Once I inquired of a little girl: "Susy, can you tell me how a Devil looks?" And her reply was: "A man without his head, but with the head of a hog." Another child, little Freddy, said that a Satan was a "serpent with four wings and a man's head." In descriptive imagery, in crude conception of a painful truth, this is not exceeded by Swedenborg, and even the New Testament contains nothing that exceeds the child's figure. Mary, a sweet little girl, described Satan as a "little, short, fat man." Another said Satan was a man "with a head somewhat like a horse." Another described it as a "flying animal that gives sicknesses to people." One said Satan is a "dragon, with power to become invisible, or to transform itself into a black cat, a butterfly, or other beautiful shapes, always transmitting evils and calamities to mankind through everything it touches." Now it is the same with nations as it is with children. Children, in their thoughts, reproduce the germs and sometimes even the forms of the religions of the creed-world.

The human bodily organs and functions are similar to a wilderness full of animals, passions, demons, and unclean spirits. Through our appetites we are all led into the wilderness to be tempted. Jesus was thus led into the wilderness. Do you remember what preceded it? Baptism! John, the zealous herald, went out preparing the way for something higher—declaring that "the kingdom of heaven was at hand." All high counselors and practical principles that go through the human spirit, are John the Baptists.

When one becomes fully prepared, physically, to enter upon the work of a new life, then the same temptations assail him that assailed Jesus. He is first tempted to over-eat! Jesus fasted. He kept from the common foods and drinks of the day. His fasting diet consisted of the simplest berries and most delicate fruit-products that grew about the wilderness. But the demon, *Hunger*, tempted him and suggested to him that "stones be made into bread." This called up the next demon, *Impatience*.

In Genesis we find the first tale of spiritual truth. It is there stated substantially that a woman prepared the dinner and then the man partook. The first Devil began his infernal work by food. It was natural and strictly appropriate for Mrs. Eve to commence house-keeping with a commendable desire to select and pre-pare such viands as would adequately tempt Mr. Adam to eat and enjoy the original "Thanksgiving dinner." According to popular orthodoxy, Adam's poor pos-terity have been more or less fools ever since.

The Devil of Appetite has clogged the functions of man's physical organization, and has sent great trouble to the hells—to the bowels, liver, stomach, and brain. Grahamites go to the other extreme. Disgusted with the Satan of Appetite, they have left his company and traveled through heaven to a very cold place beyond. After a time they return.

Suppose you draw a line, one end of which, desig-nated by A, should represent absolute evil, the center, B, a golden mean, and the other end, C, perfect good, it would, perhaps, illustrate the true life for man to lead. But one end *is not* absolute evil and the other absolute good. There is good at both extremes. Man stands enveloped in darkness, his head only looking heavenward. This is well illustrated by the garments we wear, which surround all parts of the body excepting the head. The head and face are exposed to the light and air of heaven.

Impatient persons—in their haste to jump over chasms, and because of their wish to accomplish in an hour what may certainly require a week—become irascible and angry. By their perturbed, nervous, and irritable conditions, they disturb and render unhappy those who live around them. Nature's sublime course is very different. All vast operations go on slowly. Men and women never become angels until the demon of Impatience is cast out of them.

Next comes the Satan of Anger—a mighty demon who disturbs and overturns the whole world. Behold illustrations all around. The development of this demoniac passion between boys at the street-corners, is parallel to what we read in the history of great and mighty nations. A misapprehension of words, for example, is succeeded by a quickened pulse, impatient gestures, angry looks, and then blows and a pitched battle. The spirit of Anger is instantaneously communicated from one to another, until a whole community are aroused and under the control of the demon. The demon of Impatience begets the demon of Anger. These satanic majesties become instantly manifest in the rush of blood, in the defiant attitude, and in the gleaming and savage expression of the eye. Man is truly demoniac when the evil of anger is in the ascendant.

The next evil spirit—generated from an overloaded stomach and bad digestion—is Irascibility. It is known by the absence of tranquillity and gentleness, and of sufficient patience to inquire into facts and positions;

and this condition begets Pride, which forthwith assumes the responsibility, fearlessly indorses Anger, and gives unbounded approbation and support to the deeds of Impatience.

Pride is the most powerful Satan we have to contend with. Men who have reached "the pinnacle of the temple"—who stand committed and approved as the *apex* of some station among their fellow-men—are slow to unlearn their errors and vices. The world is filled with professional characters, who are afraid to come down from the pinnacle of the commercial temple, to which they have ascended through their unrestrained Ambition. Such minds are possessed of the worst of evil spirits—Pride! The worldly ambitious man is the Prince of Darkness. He is full of unclean spirits and devils. Being afflicted with the demon of Pride, he internally declares that he would rather "rule in hell than serve in heaven." So appeareth the Prince of Rebellion in the eyes of all loyalists.

Another evil spirit, the most apparently amiable of all—a spirit of darkness appearing as an angel of light, if such a thing were possible—is the ungoverned and extravagant love of Approbation. It is the desire of Praise from those about us in the world. Those who are infested with this evil spirit, with this amiable Devil, are always standing upon the brink of a social precipice. Such minds are liable at any moment to fall and be lost. In the life of Daniel Webster we have an illustration of what was sacrificed to this evil spirit. He would have made a great and noble President over the country—an office to which he could have been elected—had the motive of his acts been a desire to do right for the sake of Right and Freedom. He was lost by his worldly efforts to win the golden opinions of too many citizens.

There are instances of "sudden conversion," where individuals have emerged from the rule of these demoniac spirits. These sudden conversions are sometimes accompanied with contortions of the counténance and writhings of the whole body. A drunkard sometimes goes suddenly to bed, driven by his great suffering. After long agony he may come out a converted and sobered sinner. Some people suppose that, on gaining the spirit-world, they will receive the baptism of absolute purification. Such are destined to sore-hearted disappointment. Those who return, teach us that all the misspent hours of life—all the seasons that have been given up to the reign of personal evils in body and mind—oppress their spirits with regrets and painful memories. Meanwhile, others, who have lived truer lives and more faithfully, walk on the shores of beautiful streams, and listen to "the tidings of great joy."

Passions and Appetites do not continue into the Summer-Land, but the effects thereof remain as adhering spheres and substances; and the post-mundane experiences arising from such imperfections are very sad. When you arrive where clean and beautiful garments are required, you may find that your wardrobe is either spotted or deficient; you may appear unlike the multitudes of those around you, and you may suffer from contrast, from a sense of unworthiness, and thus begin to realize that you have not lived out your aspirations.

To CAST OUT DEVILS.—Commence in the first place, and at once, to live in obedience to the laws written within and upon your constitution.   Some men seek to cast demons out by and through the observance of physiological laws.   Never expect to receive much mental happiness through observance of mere physiological laws ; neither attempt nor expect to be *physically* happy by observing and complying with mental laws simply.   Never be absurd.   Learn philosophy.   Apply means legitimately to the ends to be attained.   Do not seek to be angelic before your time.   Let all desire only the ripeness of full earthly progress.   Wait until stones can be pulverized into soil.   Let dull earth be matured, through all intermediate gradations, into fruit.   And, above all, never become Impatient and fret because stones are not changed into bread.   Obedience to laws of the stomach and other organs—to live as does a good fish, horse, or other animal, if pursued exclusively, even if *self* is all devoted to it—will not produce happiness in man.   That partial obedience does not complete the requirements of your being.   You possess soul, spirit, love, intellect.   It will not even suffice to cultivate your intellect exclusively, or to inform yourself upon the spiritual literature of the day, or to seek enlarged conceptions and to fellowship ennobling thoughts.   Neither of these will bring true happiness. What is needed is Equilibrium—Balance !   To purchase a farm for cultivation, you do not go either to Nova Zembla or Patagonia.   You seek naturally a clime within the temperate belt.   Never live in extremes !   Seek rather a place which comprehends and involves both extremes !   A spirit demon cannot long remain with you, or disturb your organs, when your body and soul are truly balanced. You may be tempted. But you will quickly recover and be restored to your golden position—that of a philosophical angel, a recognized Brother among the hosts of redeemed, while yet in the body. Philosophers do not believe that mankind are infested and made angry by spirits without the body. The true man knows he has the will-power to place his foot upon the head of every appetite, that he can overcome and crush all demons, within his constitution. Spiritual truths come beautifully to teach us that we can purify all the chambers of hell ; that the individual can cast out all that is evil, and unfold that spiritual harmony which shall cause his bodily wilderness to blossom as the rose.

FALSE OPINIONS.—The Churches hold that the abode of evil spirits is an external empire, and they teach that demons are persons. But the Spiritualism of the nineteenth century, as well as that of Jesus of Nazareth, brings out the clear and beautiful gospel that man contains within himself the powers of recuperation and regeneration, and teaches that the abode of unclean spirits is within. There are many who even implore protection for their appetites, and claim and expect sympathy for the condition in which they are brought by the demons that haunt them.

The human organism is full of passions and internal conflicts. The means of casting out the real demons are not prescribed in Churches or in the Medical Colleges, and yet it is a subject of far more importance than theological or simply moral teachings. \

Many and various inventions are contrived for **the**

extinction of these devils! The Jewish religion adopts a course of strict personal and national discipline. Moses seemed to see that many evils come from Tartarus, the stomach, and he laid down laws with regard to food. Discipline was the sovereign remedy. His rules were not always the laws of God, although they were given forth with the indorsement of the spirit-heaven, which he deeply realized while writing them and giving them to the people.

Curbing passions and appetites, and rigorously following Law, is what the Jews do to-day, the same as when Moses descended from Sinai with the tablets of stone. That people walk in the same old tracks, never allowing themselves to be thrown out of the grooves in which they have been running for centuries. This shows that physical and national discipline does not drive the demons out of men. The Jews are not broad-minded and liberal. Their system has not advanced them beyond the rest of mankind. The Jews of to-day are copies of the ancient people who lived in Palestine.

Jesus came among the Jews and said that the Law— or at least so much of it as did not accomplish the work of casting out demons—must be put aside forever. He announced that the laws of Moses were to be filled full of new thoughts. A new method of treatment for individual and general sins was to be adopted. He was the first graduate of all the spiritual schools—the first who really confounded the learned Doctors. Instantaneous inspiration was soon adopted as a better mode of treatment. Jesus required perfect faith. He argued that such was the remedy. The early Christians still required the work of Discipline, and Faith was the inspiration by which such discipline was to effect permanent cures. To the woman who came to him to be cured, he said, "Thy faith hath made thee whole."

Faith was and is the central gospel of the Christian world. Now let us ask whether Faith, the sovereign remedy prescribed by the Christian Church—which has been nearly two thousand years in use—has driven unclean spirits and demonic passions out of the people? The appliances of Faith have been made through Churches and other institutions at an expense beyond computation. The blood of innumerable martyrs has flowed in defense of Faith. And yet unclean spirits and demons continue to abound in men and women.

Not many persons are healed by Faith. Church-members in business and in society, are the same as persons who have not been relieved of unclean spirits. Discipline and Faith have led the world to where it now stands. Unclean spirits and demons continue to roam through mankind, bringing a horrible war upon the freest soil known on the globe. Neither Faith nor Discipline have brought men into Paradise. Both of them seem to lead large multitudes down to moral and physical damnation. To the incalculable benefits which have grown out of Discipline and Faith I do not close my eyes. I am looking—as I trust you are—from the center.

Medical systems have devised methods of relief, but they succeed only to a very small extent. Amusements are invented to lift men from the slough of despondency. With many Tobacco comes in as a palliative. Many say the happiest moments they experience in the twenty-four hours, occur during the reverie excited by a fine cigar. Thus men seek to render oblivious the influences of the evil spirits. They vainly think exter-'nal appliances will relieve them from the sufferings of internal discord. Opium is used for the same purpose. This drug is an unclean spirit which sometimes closes the mouth of the other demons. Opium is a miserable, driveling, debasing character, who stands up and re-morsely controls the whole man or woman. Doctors cannot relieve; Churches cannot. What then is the true remedy?

In a reformed state of society do you suppose that drug-stores will exist? They are so many attempts at vicarious atonement for the unclean spirits which we create and multiply every time we overstep the bounds of eating, drinking, sleeping, conjugal love, or other limits which Nature has set up within our being. True reformers see that there is another method by which these evils can be exorcised. Formerly I was disposed to be somewhat opposed to ministers. Perhaps many of you may have been a little prejudiced against them. But now, I begin to think that after all they are about as good as mechanics. But they do not cure the sin-sick any more than do physicians. When a man is a little sick, he sends for a physician; he grows worse, then he sends for a lawyer; finally, when he gets very bad, the minister is called. But all these professional appliances are but vicarious atonements—false in theory and worse in application—beautiful and mysterious quackeries, and ought to be abandoned.

There is a world of wisdom in a knowledge of inherent laws, written by the good Father and Mother

in this Book of Life—the human body and mind. All
that was said by Pythagoras, Plato, Moses, and Jesus,
may be found here. Here we may find the original of
all that has been sung, or painted, or chiseled. Progress is the law—the saving principle—by which every
end is accomplished. Men may become "masters of the
situation." Mankind can overcome all the "unclean
spirits" that roam through society, from bowels, liver,
stomach, and brain. Persons who have arrived at that
state are entitled to be styled Graduates, being prepared
to enter into the kingdom of Heaven upon Earth. Such
should be recognized—not as fanatics often are, by long
beard and uncombed hair; but by their pure and shin-
ing countenance, sweet breath, calm expression, and
general balance of character; for such minds, when in
the midst of discord and stormy passions, could say,
"Get thee behind me, Satan," and all the ugly devils
would flee away from around them. This is the
Redeemed Man—the Spiritual Graduate—a true "convert." This end is possible, and it is attainable in
this life. Will you not try to attain it?

It is an error to say that sin is a transgression of
law. No natural or divine law is ever transgressed.
Methods devised by men, and styled "laws," are not
real Divine laws. Fundamental laws are written
within us by our true parents. Ministers apprehend sin
to be a violation of statute or biblical laws. Did you
ever violate a law of your being? Never! Then, why
your sufferings? If you understand *that*, then you understand the remedy, and forthwith you may cast out
your "demons." A Christian is converted. He is a
believer in that to which he was converted. He "be-

lieves and is baptized"—a beautiful psychological law, with a germ of spiritual truth in it. Christians believe that after conversion they will be happy! Are they? They need ministers more after conversion than before. They seem to be more sick than ever. Perhaps not a demon has been driven from either bowels, liver, stomach, or brain. A family may obey all the requisitions of the Church, still they need a physician. The convert is not in harmony with the requirements of the physical laws. Laws of digestion go on the same in a dyspeptic as they do when a man is in health. The law remains in perfect action. *It* cannot be transgressed. But a man may carry his system—a part of it—beyond the requirements of other parts, and the law of digestion protests, and at that point "unclean spirits" assemble, and then what an interesting condition *he* is in for living! A walking pandemonium in the midst of sunlight, stars, and clear skies! Perhaps he has wealth, and offers one hundred dollars to his physician to make him well! Such a man cannot be made well by medicine. He cannot be placed where he will realize the requisitions of the law of digestion. He is the same miserable man notwithstanding he claims to have the "fellowship of the Holy Ghost." A good church-going farmer who does not understand agriculture, and who does not obey the requirements of the laws of seasons, cannot obtain large crops. No Christian fellowship, no priest, no prayers, can secure him a great harvest. Whilst one who never goes to church, if he comprehends and lives up to the laws of seasons, may secure bountiful supplies.

If a man is not in relation to spiritual love, by

which he is enabled to see truths as they are, he is miserable. He attends to the law of business as well as to the laws that regulate social life, and he may succeed both in business and socially. As a family man, who is a good provider, he is liked by the community. But if he does not harmonize with spiritual laws, and does not understand why truth is better for him than error, he is in a precarious position and calls for strength. If he does not harmonize with the law of conjugal love, but suffers the presence of the demon, and furnishes it with food and drink, and accepts the physician's prescription of indulgence as a remedy—as most physicians advise—and if he is spoken to from the pulpit in poetical strains and through symbolic figures, without receiving and comprehending the spiritual law, he goes to outer darkness, where he finds " weeping, and wailing, and gnashing of teeth." He has not violated the conjugal law. The mistake is, he did not come into harmony with it. Fourier taught the divinity of the passions; that they are the voices of God: and that what they prescribe it is right for men to do. He meant, I think, just what I mean when I say " love;" but as it is generally comprehended, it means yielding to the passions the right to rule the individual.

Now, here on the earth man is intended to be simply and only a healthy and happy human being: neither an animal nor an angel. The animal is past; the angel is future.

Be invariably considerate of the natural rights of others; live at home and be human; and do all things for the benefit of those around you, and for the good of all the world. *Live to a purpose*, and it will give you

majesty of position and influence. Single men and
women can only be half-persons, and the mischief is
that so many in so-called married life are but "half-
persons," performing the comic drama of conjugal love,
and continuing the vulgar farce of pretending to possess
domestic happiness. In marriage, passion and impatience oftentimes become the destroying demons.

Perhaps you have a desire to come into the relation
of a parent: this is in accordance with the law of Pa-
rental love. A full-grown person, who has not entered
upon that relation, must love something which will be
equivalent, for the time being, to a child. Many substitutes are sought and tried, and sometimes a person
will resort to that most miserable of all substitutes—a
poodle-dog. Those who do not harmonize with such
laws have constant vague. longings, and are frequently
dissatisfied with life.

If we do not develop Fraternal love, if we do not
go out from our children to visit our neighbors, and
that too for the sake of being useful to others, then we
are still under the rule of some demon. Self-love
brings in its painful limitations. These are the natural
punishments which come to all who live for themselves
alone. Very selfish persons are always miserable.
Seek to know and truly love a Principle, and not give
rein to your passions, which are demons. Each may
be a sun which can shine effulgently on other orbs—on
a child, a sister, brother, neighbors, or on other persons about you—and their reciprocations will be ever
promotive of joy and spiritual satisfaction.

The sure way to Grow is to come first into strict
harmony with the laws that regulate the body, then

seek to fulfill those which regulate the mind. Commence with the stomach and do not over-eat. Learn that all that disturbs the physical nature disturbs the inward harmony. Never live wholly for yourself. Whatever purpose you live for, let it be sacred to your heart, and it will dignify and save you. Then heavenly whisperings will come to you, which will make you realize, that although you are strictly human, nevertheless you are but little lower than the angels.

PROGRESSIVE BOOK DEPOSITORY,

AT THE OFFICE OF THE

HERALD OF PROGRESS,

274 Canal Street, New York.

Messrs. A. J. DAVIS & Co. keep constantly on hand, or will supply at short notice, all the most valuable PROGRESSIVE PUBLICATIONS of the day.

Special attention is given to the departments of Spiritual Philosophy and Reform, in which their Catalogue will embrace all the standard works procurable in this country.

To the following list may be added all approved Anti-Slavery Books, works on Phrenology, Temperance, Health, and Land Reform. Also, publications devoted to the Elevation of Woman, to Physical Education, Social Progress, and Liberal Principles in Theology.

☞ Orders from California and Oregon should provide for double Postage.

WORKS BY ANDREW JACKSON DAVIS.

	PRICE.	POST.
THE PRINCIPLES OF NATURE: Her Divine Revelations, and a Voice to Mankind. 1 vol. 8vo. 800 pages,	$2 00	44

THE GREAT HARMONIA: Being a Philosophical Revelation of the Natural, Spiritual, and Celestial Universe. In Five Distinct Volumes, (12mo.) as follows:

VOL. I.—THE PHYSICIAN. | VOL. III.—THE SEER.
VOL. II.—THE TEACHER. | VOL. IV.—THE REFORMER.
VOL. V.—THE THINKER.

	PRICE.	POST.
Per volume,	1 00	20
THE MAGIC STAFF. An Autobiography. By Andrew Jackson Davis. 550 pages, 12mo,	1 00	23
THE PENETRALIA: Being Harmonial Answers to Important Questions,	1 00	22
ANSWERS TO EVER-RECURRING QUESTIONS from the People. A Sequel to the Penetralia. 1 vol. 12mo, 400 pages,	1 00	18

PRICE. POST.

THE HARBINGER OF HEALTH: Containing Medical Prescriptions for the Human Body and Mind. 1 vol. 12mo, 428 pages, - - - - - - - 1 00 20
THE PHILOSOPHY OF SPIRIT INTERCOURSE: An Explanation of Modern Mysteries. Cloth, 75. Paper, 50 06
THE PRESENT AGE AND INNER LIFE: A Sequel to Spiritual Intercourse, - - - - - 75 15
THE HISTORY AND PHILOSOPHY OF EVIL—With Suggestions for more Ennobling Institutions and Systems of Education. Cloth 50 cts. Paper, - - - 30 08
THE HARMONIAL MAN; or *Thoughts for the Age.* Paper, 30 06
THE PHILOSOPHY OF SPECIAL PROVIDENCES: A Vision. Paper, - - - - - - - 15 03
FREE THOUGHTS CONCERNING RELIGION; or, *Nature vs. Theology.* - - - - - - - 15 03
THE APPROACHING CRISIS. Out of Print.

WORKS BY OTHER AUTHORS.

ARCANA OF NATURE: or, The History and Laws of Creation. By Hudson Tuttle, - - - - - 1 00 16
A. B. C of Life. By Dr. A. B. Child, - - - - 25 03
ANSWER TO CHARGES OF BELIEF IN MODERN REVELATIONS. &c. By Mr. and Mrs. A. E. Newton, 10 01
AMERICA AND HER DESTINY. A Lecture delivered by Emma Hardinge, - - - - - - - 05 01
ARGUMENTS ON STATE RIGHTS AND POPULAR SOVEREIGNTY, Examined and Refuted. By S. B. Brittan, - - - - - - - - - 05 01
AMERICAN CRISIS: or, the Trial and Triumph of Democracy. By Warren Chase, - - - - 20 3
BOUQUET OF SPIRITUAL FLOWERS. Received Chiefly through the mediumship of Mrs. J. S. Adams. 75 cents, $1 00. and $1 50, according to the style of the binding. 12
BIBLE THE: Is it of Divine Origin, Authority and Influence? By S. J. Finney. 25 cents. Cloth. - - - 40 05
COMMUNICATIONS FROM THE SPIRIT WORLD. Given by Lorenzo Dow and others, - - - - 25 05
CATECHISM OF THE HISTORY AND TEACHINGS OF THE BIBLE. By a Searcher after Truth, - - 10 01
DISSERTATION ON THE EVIDENCE OF INSPIRATION. By Datus Kelly, - - - - - - - 15 03
DISCUSSION OF MODERN SPIRITUALISM, between Prof. J. Stanley Grimes and Leo Miller, Esq. Pamphlet, 170 pages, - - - - - - - - - 15 03
DISCUSSION OF SPIRITUALISM AND IMMORTALITY, between Elder Miles Grant and Rev. J. S. Loveland, 10 03
DEALINGS WITH THE DEAD; The Human Soul, its Migrations and its Trans-Migrations. By P. B. Randolph. 75 10
DIVORCE. A Correspondence between Horace Greeley and Robert Dale Owen, with the Divorce Laws of New York and Indiana. 60 pages, - - - - - 10 01

PRICE. POST.

ELECTRICAL PSYCHOLOGY. Philosophy of, in twelve Lectures. By Dr J. B. Dods. Muslin, 75. Paper,   50   12

EVIDENCES OF MODERN SPIRITUALISM Being a Debate held at Decatur, Mich., between A. B. Whiting and Rev. Jo eph Jones. - - - - - - -   30   05

ESSAYS ON VARIOUS SUBJECTS. Intended to elucidate the Causes of the Changes coming upon all the Earth at the present time. Given through a Lady, 50 cents. Postage, 10. Cloth, - - - -   75   15

EYE OPENER; or, *Catholicism Unmasked.* By a Catholic Priest. Containing " Doubts of Infidels," embodying thirty important Questions to the Clergy; also. forty close questions to the Doctors of Divinity, by Zepa, &c. - - -   40   06

FUGITIVE WIFE. By Warren Chase. 25 cts. Cloth,   40   05

GUIDE OF WISDOM AND KNOWLEDGE TO THE SPIRIT WORLD. By Almond J. Packard, - -   10   01

FOOTFALLS ON THE BOUNDARY OF ANOTHER WORLD. By Robert Dale Owen, - - - - 1 25   25

FURTHER COMMUNICATIONS FROM THE WORLD OF SPIRITS, on subjects highly important to the human family. Given through a Lady. 50 cents. postage 10. Cloth, - - - - - - - - -   75   15

FAMILIAR SPIRITS, and Spiritual Manifestations; being a series of articles by Dr Enoch Pond. Professor in the Bangor Theological Seminary, with a Reply, by A Bingham, Esq., of Boston, - - - - -   15   03

GREAT. CONFLICT; or, Cause and Cure of Secession. By Leo Miller, Esq., delivered at Pratt's Hall, Providence, R. I., - - - - - - - - - -   10   01

HAND-BOOK OF STANDARD PHONOGRAPHY. "A Complete Self-Instructor." By Andrew J. Graham, 1 00   25

HIEROPHANT; or, *Gleanings from the Past.* Being an Exposition of Biblical Astronomy, &c., &c. By G. C. Stewart. 16mo. 234 pages, - - - - - -   75   10

HONEST MAN'S BOOK OF FINANCE AND POLITICS, - - - - - - - - -   50   09

HEALING OF THE NATIONS. Given through Charles Linton. With an Introduction and Appendix. By Gov. Talmadge. 550 pages, - - - - - 1 50   30

KISS FOR A BLOW; or, Stories for Children. By H. C. Wright. 38 cents. Illustrated, - - - -   50   10

LIFE LINE OF THE LONE ONE. By Warren Chase,   75   15

LEGALIZED PROSTITUTION; or, Marriage as it is. and Marriage as it should be. Philosophically Considered. By Charles S Woodruff, M. D., - - - -   75   15

LETTER TO THE CHESTNUT STREET CONGREGATIONAL CHURCH, Chelsea, Mass., in Reply to its charges of having become a Reproach to the Cause of Truth, in consequence of a Change of Religious Belief. By John S. Adams, - - - - - - - -   15   03

LOVE AND MOCK LOVE; or, How to Marry to Conjugal Satisfaction. By Geo. Stearns, - - - -   25   03

PRICE. POST.

MARRIAGE AND PARENTAGE; or, *The Reproductive Element in Man as a Means to his Elevation and Happiness.*
By Henry C. Wright, - - - - - 1 00 18

NEW TESTAMENT MIRACLES. and Modern Miracles. The comparative amount of evidence for each—the nature of both; testimony of a hundred witnesses. An Essay read before the Divinity School. Cambridge. By J. H. Fowler, 30 05

MORAL AND RELIGIOUS STORIES; or Scripture Illustrated. A Book for Little Children. By Mrs. M. L. Willis, - - - - - - - - .- - 15 01

"MINISTRY OF ANGELS" REALIZED. A Letter to the Edwards Congregational Church, Boston. By A. E. Newton, - - - - - - - - 15 01

OPTIMISM THE LESSON OF AGES. By Benjamin Blood, 60 10

ODIC-MAGNETIC LETTERS OF BARON REICHENBACH. Translated from the German, by John S Hittell, - - - - - - - - 25 06

PHILOSOPHY OF CREATION. By Thomas Paine: through Horace G. Wood, Medium. Cloth. 40 cts. Paper, 25 05

PHYSICO-PHYSIOLOGICAL RESEARCHES. By Baron Chas. Von Reichenbach, - - - - - 1 00 00

PROGRESSIVE LIFE OF SPIRITS AFTER DEATH, as given in Spiritual Communications to, and with Introduction and Notes by A. B. Child, 15 01

PSALMS OF LIFE. A Compilation of Psalms, Hymns, Chants, and Anthems. &c., embodying the Spiritual, Progressive, and Reformatory Sentiment of the Present Age. By John S. Adams, - - - - - 75 15

PSYCHOLOGY; or, *The Science of the Soul* By Joseph Haddock M. D. Illustrated, - - - - 25 05

PRE-ADAMITE MAN. The Story of the Human Race, from 35 000 to 100 000 years ago. By Griffin Lee, of Texas, 1 25 25

RECENT INQUIRIES IN THEOLOGY. By eminent English Churchmen, Dr. Temple. Rowland Williams, Baden Powell, Jewett, &c Being "Essays and Reviews," reprinted from the second London edition. 12mo, - 1 25 20

RELIGION AND MORALITY. A Criticism on the Jewish Jehovah, Patriarchs. Prophets, early Church Fathers, modern Church Leaders, &c, - - - - 30 05

ROAD TO SPIRITUALISM. Being a Series of Four Lectures delivered by Dr R. T. Hallock, - - - 18 03

RELIGION OF MANHOOD; or, The Age of Thought. By Dr J. H. Robinson, - - - - - - 75 10

REPORT OF AN EXTRAORDINARY CHURCH-TRIAL; Conservatives *versus* Progressives. By Philo Hermes, 15 01

SELF-CONTRADICTIONS OF THE BIBLE. 144 Propositions. Proved Affirmatively and Negatively by Quotations from Scripture, without comment. Cloth, 33 cts Paper, 15 pd

SPIRIT WORKS REAL, BUT NOT MIRACULOUS. A Lecture by Allen Putnam. - - - - 25 03

SCENES IN THE SPIRIT WORLD; or, Life in the Spheres. By Hudson Tuttle, Medium. Paper, - - - 25 05

A NEW JOURNAL OF REFORM.

THE HERALD OF PROGRESS.

ANDREW JACKSON DAVIS, Editor.

Assisted by an Association of Able Writers and Correspondents.

A FIRST CLASS FAMILY NEWSPAPER,

NOT DEVOTED TO ONE IDEA.

The attention of all reformatory, progressive, and spiritual minds, is invited to the distinctive features of the HERALD OF PROGRESS. *Among the many departments of thought represented are:*

QUESTIONS AND ANSWERS.—Over this Department the EDITOR exclusively presides. The people forward their peculiar questions, and the "Answer" is given from the light of the "Superior.Condition," in a candid and fraternal spirit.

WHISPERINGS TO CORRESPONDENTS.—In which will be given many laconic inspirations and practical hints for the benefit of individuals.

VOICES FROM THE PEOPLE.—This department is designed to bring the free thoughts of the People before the world, thus assisting our readers to a knowledge of the true pulse of the nation.

SPIRIT MYSTERIES.—Under this head we publish the most authentic Facts, and the best attested manifestations in proof of individual immortality, so that the thinking world may stand upon a *scientific* basis in matters of religion.

BROTHERHOOD.—In which name will be advocated and chronicled those rights and movements whereby the best interests of humanity are explained and promoted.

CHILDHOOD.—Furnishing attractive reading for the Young, so that the children of all families may learn to live wisely. happily, and long on the earth.

PULPIT AND ROSTRUM.—Containing sketches of Spiritual discourses, reports of Sermons favorable to progress and reform, abstracts of Lectures, and matters of interest concerning individual Workers in the field of Thought.

DOINGS OF THE MORAL POLICE—Under this head we publish the "Doings" of those who perform acts of benevolence and heroism in behalf of the unfortunate and oppressed; in contradistinction to the *demoralizing* reports of Murders, Robberies, and deeds of blood, with which many newspapers abound.

MEDICAL WHISPERS.—This important "hospital" department is filled by the medical contributions of the EDITOR. Although the physiological instructions are given in reply to correspondents, yet the "Whispers" are designed to be sufficiently general to comprehend and cure a multitude of the ills of the diseased and suffering.

TERMS OF SUBSCRIPTION.

THE HERALD OF PROGRESS is published weekly, on a double folio of eight pages, for two dollars per annum, or one dollar for six months, payable in advance To Clubs, three copies to one post-office, $5; ten copies, $16; twenty copies, $30.

☞ Specimen numbers sent free. Address

A. J. DAVIS & CO., Publishers,

274 Canal Street, New York.

CPSIA information can be obtained
at www.ICGtesting.com
Printed in the USA
BVHW04*1201060818
523683BV00013B/116/P